GENE PERRET

Growing Older is So Much Fun EVERYBODY'S Doing It

COVER ILLUSTRATION BY
JAMES R. SHEPHERD

FLIP-BOOK ILLUSTRATIONS BY
VICKY SNOW

WitWorks™

WitWorks™

A funny little division of Arizona Highways Books
2039 West Lewis Avenue, Phoenix, Arizona 85009.
Telephone: (602) 712-2200
Website: www.witworksbooks.com

Publisher — Win Holden
Managing Editor — Bob Albano
Associate Editor — Evelyn Howell
Art Director — Mary Winkelman Velgos
Photography Director — Peter Ensenberger
Production Director — Cindy Mackey

Library of Congress Catalog Number 99-068960
ISBN 1-893860-10-8

Growing Older is So Much Fun EVERYBODY'S Doing It
First edition published in 2000. Second Printing, 2000.
Printed in the United States.
Book Designer — Mary Winkelman Velgos

Like
good wine, I
keep getting better
with age . . . except
I don't have to
lie upside down
in a cellar
to do it.

The trouble
with experience
is that by the time
you get it,
the younger folks
tell you to keep
it to yourself.

GETTING CROTCHETY

IS NATURE'S WAY

OF REWARDING YOU

FOR GROWING

OLDER.

Age before beauty
is a nice thought,
but I've learned
not to depend on it
when I come to
a 4-way stop sign.

*My hearing's
not bad.
It's just that
folks today
don't say much
that's worth
listening to.*

I DON'T

WANT

TO ACT

MY AGE.

I WANT

TO ACT

YOUR AGE.

Sure, parts of me ache
. . . but parts of me
are still having fun
after all these years, too.

With age comes wisdom. That's not true, but the younger folks aren't wise enough yet to know that.

Have I

SLOWED DOWN

OR HAVE I JUST

COME TO REALIZE

THAT EVERYONE ELSE

IS MOVING

TOO DARN FAST?

IF I'M NOT
GROWING OLD
GRACEFULLY, THAT'S
YOUR PROBLEM,
ISN'T IT?

We older folks have a good thing going. Have you ever noticed it's always your elders who are telling you to respect your elders?

I was just as wise
when I was young
as I am now.
It just took me
all these years
to realize it.

MY MEMORY

MAY BE FAILING,

BUT WITH A

PAST LIKE MINE,

THAT MAY NOT

BE SO BAD.

Young people have
dreams; old people
have memories.
Many of the dreams will
never happen, but
a lot of the memories
never happened, either.

*If I knew then
what I know now,
I would have
been even more
unbearable
than I actually was.*

YES, I DOZE OFF

OCCASIONALLY.

SOMETIMES I

PREFER OBLIVION

TO THE COMPANY.

Remember this:
Nobody does anything
for an older person
that an older person
didn't once do
for a younger person.

*There are some
things I can't
do anymore.
On the other hand,
there are a lot of
things I've already
done and don't ever
want to do again.*

We're supposed to get smarter as we get older, but don't bank on it. I've got some old friends who are still dumb.

I can hear
everything I want to
hear or need to hear.
That's why I keep
saying "What?"
to you so much.

THERE IS NO
"BEST" AGE IN LIFE.
THERE'S ONLY
PUTTING THE BEST LIFE
INTO YOUR AGE.

*There's
nothing wrong
with needing
reading glasses
to read.
You need a
drinking glass
to drink,
don't you?*

I do some of the same
dumb things now that
I did when I was young
. . . only now people
blame them on my age.

It's not that
as you get older
you get smarter.
It's just that
fewer and fewer
people bother to
contradict you.

*As I grow older
it becomes
easier and easier
for me to voice
my own opinion
and harder and
harder for me to
hear yours.*

I did some
dumb things when I
was young, but I don't
do them anymore.
I don't have to.
There're enough
young people around
doing them for me.

I'VE BECOME

IMPULSIVE

IN MY OLDER YEARS.

EVERY TIME

I TRY TO THINK

BEFORE I ACT,

I DOZE OFF.

*If I had my life
to live over again,
I wouldn't do it.
I got through youth
once without
hurting myself.
I don't want
to press my luck.*

I LOOK ON IT

THIS WAY — AGE IS

A PROMOTION FROM

YOUTH.

I'm not so nimble
anymore, but I don't care.
I was nimble
when I was 20, but
I didn't know
what the word meant
until I was 30.

IF OLDER PEOPLE
ARE SUPPOSED TO BE
FORGETFUL,
HOW COME THERE
ARE SO MANY
CONVENTIONS WITH
YOUNGER PEOPLE
WEARING NAMETAGS?

A "has been"
is a
far cry better
than a
"never gonna be."

There's not much
difference between
being young and
being old, except that
being old
takes longer.

I DON'T HAVE

BAD HEARING;

I HAVE

SELECTIVE HEARING.

AND YOU'RE

NOT PART OF

MY SELECTION.

I've left my footprints
in the sands of time.
Now I just want to leave
my behind print in this
old easy chair.

*Don't try
to change my mind.
Chances are
I've been wrong
longer than you've
been alive.*

Just because we're older doesn't mean we can't have fun. We can still get together every once in a while and paint the town gray.

So WHAT IF I MOVE A

LITTLE SLOWER?

I'LL JUST GO

TO PLACES THAT ARE

CLOSER TO ME.

The older
one gets, the less
appealing
lifetime
guarantees are.

There are a lot
of things I don't do as
well as I once did.
But there are also
a few things
I'm doing better
than I ever hoped.

Longevity becomes

real fun when

your children

start acting older

than you do.

M<small>Y GOAL</small>

<small>HAS ALWAYS BEEN</small>

<small>TO LIVE FOREVER.</small>

S<small>O FAR, SO GOOD.</small>

They've got devices to help bad hearing. But nothing's ever going to help bad listening.

You know how we get
wiser as we get older?
By learning that
when we were younger we
didn't know nearly
as much as
we thought we did.

We make a lot of mistakes when we're young . . . so we can enjoy them when we get older.

Young people
have dreams;
older folks have
memories.
The real blessing
is that we both
have now.

*I'm the same me
I was when
I was younger.
It's just that
the container
I keep it in
is getting a
little weathered.*

DON'T WORRY

ABOUT ME.

I'M AS YOUNG AS

MY MEMORIES . . . AND

I'VE YET TO SEE

A MEMORY WITH

WRINKLES.

With age comes wisdom — and a lot of other things with medical names attached to them.

I LIKE

TO BROWSE

IN ANTIQUE

STORES . . . AND

VISIT WITH

OLD FRIENDS.

The perfect age is when you can wear your most comfortable shoes with any outfit.

I USED TO SAY

"IF I KNEW THEN WHAT

I KNOW NOW."

THEN IT DAWNED ON

ME THAT I KNEW

IT THEN;

I JUST CHOSE TO

IGNORE IT.

God grant me the courage to do those things I can do; the patience to accept those things I can't do; and a good doctor who can tell me the difference.

We don't get wiser
as we get older.
We still do dumb
things; we just have
more people making
excuses for us.

As you get older,
your IQ gets a little
higher . . . but
everything else on
your body gets
a little lower.

RETIREMENT

IS WHEN YOU KICK

BACK AND DO

NOTHING.

IT'S LIKE RECESS FOR

SENIOR CITIZENS.

My memory has
actually improved
over time.
I can now remember
a lot of things
that never even
happened.

It's human nature
for husbands and wives
to grow old together.
It's just that husbands
do it much faster.

WHEN I WAS YOUNG,

I WAS UNPLEASANT.

NOW THAT I'M OLDER,

I'M "FEISTY."

The only difference between dating in your teens and dating in your later years is that when you were a teenager, it was your car that ran out of gas, not you.

*It's just not fair.
Beauty is in the
eye of the beholder,
but your age
is spelled out
on your driver's
license.*

I don't long for the
good old days.
I'm too busy trying
to create some
good new days.

I CAN STILL KICK UP

MY HEELS.

IT'S JUST THAT

THE LANDING HURTS

A LITTLE MORE NOW.

AGE IS

A NUMBER.

OLD AGE IS

A MENTALITY.

I don't lie
about my age.
But I do enjoy lying
about my youth.

I've still got one
good punch left in me
and I may use it on
the next person who
calls me "spry."

Ｈow can people

who don't know

my age tell me

I don't look my age?

After you reach a
certain age, the
government pays you
for doing nothing.
That's what my taxes
did for them for years.

You don't really get
smarter as you
get older;
you just come
to realize
there are a lot more
people dumber
than you are.

IN YOUNGER PEOPLE

IT'S EFFERVESCENCE.

IN OLDER FOLKS

IT'S JUST GAS.

If I had my life
to live over again,
I'd do everything
the same . . . but I'd
have to have
a little nap first.

*I'm enjoying
my older years.
I'm looking
at life through
rose-colored
reading glasses.*

I NOW ENJOY THE
SIMPLE PLEASURES,
WHICH IS ANYTHING
THAT'S FUN AND
DOESN'T HURT
AFTERWARD.

It took me a while

to learn that age

is a number,

not an excuse.

Keep plugging.
If you can't shoot your
age in golf,
take up bowling.

So what if I'm not
a kid anymore?
I can still have fun
with some other
old goats.

*Senior citizens
can still be powerful.
Look at God.
He's older
than all of us.*

The beauty of aging:
The older you get,
the longer you've
enjoyed your
friends.

I have a lot in common
with my grandchildren.
They've never heard of
most of the things
I've forgotten about.

Maybe Jimmy Durante said it best: "If I had known I was going to live this long, I would have taken better care of myself."

Older folks

can still

chase after an

attractive member

of the opposite sex.

We just try not

to do it on hills.

I don't mind
using a few tricks
to keep myself
looking young.
When I get up
each morning
"some assembly
is required."

It's easier to behave when you're older. After a certain age, some of the Ten Commandments become unbreakable.

Don't

UNDERESTIMATE

OLDER FOLKS.

MICHAEL JORDAN

RETIRED WHEN HE

WAS 35, BUT HE

CAN STILL DRIBBLE.

If it weren't for us
older people,
Boy Scouts would have
to help each other
across the street.

*We all get older.
It's just that some
of us do it younger
than others.*

MY HEARING'S

GOING. MY EYESIGHT'S

GOING. BUT DON'T

FORGET THAT

I'M STILL GOING, TOO.

I'VE ALWAYS ENJOYED

ANTIQUES —

ESPECIALLY

NOW THAT

I'VE BECOME ONE.

Think about this: Maybe I heard you and I'm just choosing to ignore what you said.

WE OLDER FOLKS

HAVE A PURPOSE

IN LIFE.

IF NOTHING ELSE,

WE MAKE

MIDDLE-AGED PEOPLE

FEEL YOUNGER.

The same folks

who patiently hold

the door open for me

beep their horns when

they're behind me

on the freeway.

It's not that my memory's failing. It's just that I've done a lot of things that aren't worth remembering.

My bones may ache
and my muscles get sore,
but remember, thinking
doesn't require
any moving parts.

Is my memory failing
or am I just discarding
some old memories
to make room
for some new ones?

I'VE FOUND THAT
A FEW OLD FOLKS
CAN'T HEAR,
BUT A LOT OF
YOUNG FOLKS
CAN'T LISTEN.

I can't do a lot of
things I used to do,
but then many of them
I never should have
done in the first place.

I've still got
places to go and
people to see, but
a few of them
are going to have
to meet me half way.

*I always say,
"Respect your elders
or risk a
nasty cane bump
on your head."*

My mother always taught me to respect my elders, but I can loosen up a bit now that I don't have any.

I'VE SLOWED

DOWN A BIT.

THAT'S WHY

I ONLY GO

TO PLACES

I REALLY WANT TO BE.

I hate when young
people patronize me.
I've been young
a lot longer
than they have.

I MADE

MANY MISTAKES WHEN

I WAS YOUNG.

THE ONES THAT WERE

FUN I HOPE TO

MAKE AGAIN.

*I don't move
so fast anymore
because anywhere
I'm going
I've already been.*

One nice thing
about growing old
is that I can pretend
I don't hear you.

I'M YOUNG

AT HEART . . . AND

A FEW OTHER

SELECT BODY PARTS.

The problem with
going through your
second childhood is
that everybody wants
to be your parent.

Now that

I'M OLD ENOUGH

TO DO WHATEVER

I PLEASE,

NOTHING

PLEASES ME.

*After you reach
a certain age,
you don't have to
think before you act.
In fact, you don't
even have to act.*

Don't tell me I look
good for my age.
That's like saying,
"You're pretty smart
for someone with
your limited IQ."

I'm proud
of my wrinkles.
The only outfit that
doesn't have wrinkles
is the one that
does nothing but
hang in the closet.

*The golden years
are when your dreams
can come true — if
you can remember
what they are.*

It's just not right.
When you're young,
you're young
and carefree;
but when you're old,
you're just old.

SOME PEOPLE

WHO ARE YOUNG

AND FOOLISH DON'T

GET OLDER AND WISER.

THEY JUST GET OLDER

AND MORE

EXPERIENCED

AT BEING FOOLISH.

*The best things
in life are free,
which bothers me.
It means I don't get
my senior citizen
discount.*

You know why you
can't teach an old dog
new tricks?
Because the old dog
is probably smarter
than you are.

You DON'T HAVE

TO GET CROTCHETY

AS YOU GROW

OLDER — ONLY

IF YOU'RE

DOING IT RIGHT.

When I was young
my mother told me
what I shouldn't do.
Now my doctor does.

I may not look as good
as I used to, but the people
I want to look good for
can't see as well as they
used to, either.

I FEEL I'M

PRETTY SMART

FOR HAVING SURVIVED

ALL THE DUMB

THINGS I'VE DONE.

It's harder to

have fun

when you're older.

There're too many

young people

telling you

it's not good

for you.

*It's good to laugh
when you're older —
even if it's at
what you did
when you were
younger.*

ANYONE WHO'S

LIVED WITHOUT

MAKING SOME

MISTAKES

HASN'T

REALLY LIVED.

Money is nice,
but health is better.
You don't have to leave
your health to someone
after you're gone.

Have some fun

while you're young.

After a certain age,

your kids,

your budget or

your doctor

won't let you.

Older folks remember
what it's like
to be young.
Younger folks can only
guess what it's like
to be older.

I don't really care if my
hearing's going.
The only thing people
say to me anymore is,
"Have you taken
your medicine?"

I'M NOT ONE

TO TAKE

ADVICE FROM

YOUNGER FOLKS.

THERE'S NOTHING

THEY CAN DO THAT I

CAN'T DO — OR

HAVEN'T

ALREADY DONE.

YES, I DO FORGET

NAMES AND FACES,

BUT HAVE YOU EVER

CONSIDERED IT MAY

BE FOR GOOD CAUSE?

I do move a bit
more slowly now.
That's because
after you've been
everywhere, you
find out that
not much of it
was worth rushing to.

*A hearing aid
is a real godsend.
I can turn it
and you off
at the same time.*

AGE IS RELATIVE.
THERE'S ONLY ONE
PERSON IN THE WORLD
WHO ISN'T YOUNGER
THAN SOMEBODY.

The clerk said,
"Are you a senior citizen?"
I said, "If you have to ask,
your eyesight must be
worse than mine."

Y OU'RE

ONLY YOUNG ONCE,

BUT IF YOU USE

YOUR HEAD, IT CAN

LAST A LIFETIME.

Now that
I've got a new
hearing aid,
try saying something
intelligent
for a change.

WHAT I CALL

NOSTALGIA,

A LOT OF PEOPLE

CALL HISTORY.

They say that old folks have their memories. I've got news for them — I've got memories that haven't even happened yet.

I'VE GOT MUCH MORE

EXPERIENCE THAN YOU.

SO WHEN I WANT

YOUR OPINION, I'LL

GIVE IT TO YOU.

Figuratively speaking,
I've been around
the block a few times.
I don't need suggestions
from people who aren't
allowed to cross the street.

WHEN YOU KNOW

AS MUCH AS I DO,

YOU'LL KNOW

ENOUGH TO KEEP IT

TO YOURSELF.

I DO EXERCISE.

I TAKE A GOOD,

BRISK NAP

TWO OR

THREE TIMES

A DAY.

When my
long-term memory is
working, my short-term
memory fails.
When my short-term
memory is working,
my long-term
memory fails.
When both my long-term
and my short-term
memories are working,
I blow out all the fuses
in the house.

*I must
look older
than I thought.
My granddaughter
asked me to draw
a picture of
a dinosaur — from
memory.*